Guide to the w
'Amsterdam' 1749 at Hastings

By Peter Marsden

Published 2007

Printed by Cliffe Enterprise, Eastbourne
www.cliffe-enterprise.com

© Nautical Museums Trust
Shipwreck & Coastal Heritage Centre
Rock-a-Nore Road, Hastings TN34 3DW

01424 437452

www.shipwreck-heritage.org.uk

Cover image: 'Visitors exploring the wreck of the Amsterdam'

4

Map by J. Speed c. 1610 showing a strange island near Bulverhythe. This is one of the earliest maps of the Hastings area

Visitors at the wreck of the Amsterdam

The maritime shore in the Hastings area contains a combination of heritage features that is unique in Britain, and tells an impressive story that straddles a huge expanse of time. All of this comes together at Bulverhythe, on the boundary between Hastings and Bexhill, where at low tide you can clamber over rocks that preserve the fossil remains of the age of the dinosaurs 135 million years ago. Then you can wander into a semi-submerged prehistoric forest 4000 years old, before exploring the sunken hull of the two-thirds complete wreck of the Dutch merchant ship Amsterdam, run ashore in 1749 and swallowed by the beach. So important is this historic shipwreck that it is protected as an historic monument by English Heritage. In addition, the shingle beach is an important habitat for rare plants, such as Sea Kale and the Yellow Horned Poppy, which have adapted to this harsh environment.

This coast has been constantly changing as the rising sea level, caused by global warming, threatens to flood homes and businesses. Consequently, dramatic modern sea defences have been constructed by the Environment Agency.

Archaeologists, historians and botanists have combined to study this unique group of maritime features that are free for everyone to visit, and are being included in the Pebsham Countryside Park that also embraces a huge area of natural countryside in the Combe Haven valley. Thanks to the Environment Agency the shore at Bulverhythe is laid out for visitors, with a viewing platform and information boards, and stairways giving safe access to the beach through the sea defences at low tide. You will also find the full story of the maritime shore, with many of its historic treasures displayed, at the Shipwreck & Coastal Heritage Centre in Rock-a-Nore Road, at the rear of Hastings harbour.

Funding from the Local Heritage Initiative and the Environment Agency has made the interpretation of the shore possible, with the support of Hastings Borough Council, Rother District Council, East Sussex County Council and English Heritage.

Exploring the Bulverhythe beach

The Bulverhythe heritage shore is reached from Hastings and Bexhill by car and bus along the Bexhill Road, the A259. Since pedestrian access to the beach from Bexhill Road is restricted by the coastal railway line, the best route is to walk down Bridge Way (where car parking is not permitted), and then onto the footbridge over the railway.

There is always something special to see on the beach at low tide, but the lowest monthly spring tides are best. These occur in the mornings and evenings during the few days following New Moon and Full Moon. The wreck of the Amsterdam is normally visible when local tide tables give low tide as below 1m above Chart Datum. Please contact the Shipwreck & Coastal Heritage Centre for advice on the best dates to visit the heritage shore.

As tides and currents are always modifying the blanket of sand on the beach, there is no guarantee about what you will see. The winter gales often expose features, but the gentle summer tides tend to spread sand and obscure them.

The beach is normally safe for all the family, though boots and warm clothing are desirable in the evenings. A word of caution is needed: please do not climb on the sea defences as they are dangerous and have deep cavities between the massive blocks of stone. Also, the natural rock outcrops on the beach are slippery, and around the Amsterdam there can be pools of water of varying depth, and patches of quicksand occur particularly around her bow (the end nearest the shore). Being sensible is all that is needed to enjoy a fascinating hour or two as the sea rolls back at low tide to reveal a unique 135 million years old maritime story.

Now let us begin our exploration.

A guided tour assembling at the end of Bridge Way

Left: Studying the prehistoric forest of 2000 BC at Bulverhythe in 2007

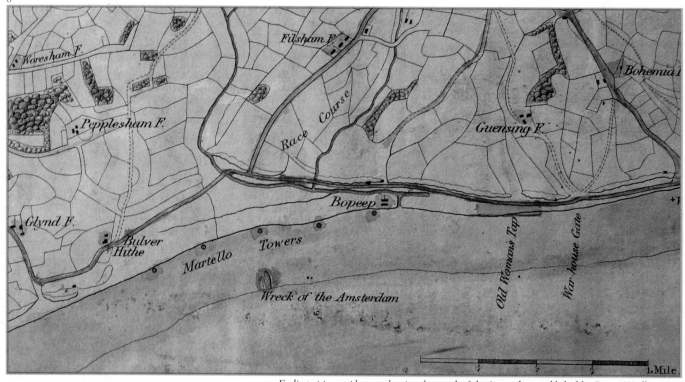

Earliest visitor guide map showing the wreck of the Amsterdam, published by George Wooll in 1827

The changing coastline

The starting point for exploring the beach is the seaward end of the footbridge from Bridge Way where it crosses the coastal railway. There have been major changes to this coast for thousands of years, as the rising sea level following the Ice Age has caused erosion and flooding. To the east of Bulverhythe the historic Cinque Port of Hastings was partly washed away in storms during the thirteenth century, and erosion formed the sandstone cliffs on which the medieval castle now stands.

Throughout recent centuries, the beach at Bulverhythe has been a windswept river valley between low sandstone hills, of which Little Galley Hill is a remnant. The small river Asten flows down the Combe Haven valley, and long ago when the sea level was much lower the valley extended under the present beach, but as the sea has risen the prevailing eastward current has blocked the mouth of the valley with a gravel beach and has forced the river Asten eastwards to enter the sea at Bo-Peep. The earliest detailed map of Bulverhythe dates from around 1750 and shows Bo-Peep, now the name of a pub. This was probably a smugglers'

landing place for contraband. The popular nursery rhyme refers to smugglers (the 'sheep') and to the Customs men ('Bo-Peep'), and to the contraband ('tails').

Erosion has been incessant here, and the sea has even destroyed a series of massive round Martello towers built on the beach as recent as 1805. Each of these had a large gun on top as a defence against a French invasion by Napoleon.

Nineteenth century picture showing the Martello Tower opposite the wreck of the Amsterdam, collapsing from erosion by the sea

Left: Spraying gravel onto the sea defences in 2005

Right: Sea erosion was dangerously close to the railway before the latest sea defences were built by the Environment Agency

The sea defences

The global warming that has been melting the ice caps of the world since the Ice Age ended about 12,000 years ago, is responsible for raising the sea level, and nowadays the sea threatens to break through the gravel beach to flood over 750 homes and businesses in the low-lying Combe Haven valley. The A259 coast road and miles of low lying farmland would be inundated, the coastal railway line would be broken, and the main sewage system for the area would be lost.

By 2005 the danger had become so serious that new sea defences were constructed by the Environment Agency across the marshy bottom of the Combe Haven valley. They replaced earlier sea defences, and required 100,000 tonnes of rock to be delivered by sea from Norway, and 50,000 tonnes of shingle used as a reinforcement.

Hundreds of homes are now safe – but only for a while. Global warming is continuing and the sea level is still rising so that in time the sea defences will have to be extended.

The sea defences and, in the beach, the Cretaceous rocks from the Age of the Dinosaurs

Reconstruction of the head of an Iguanadon dinosaur

Fossil beach ripples in the rocks at Bulverhythe, 135m years old

Sketch reconstruction of an Iguanodon (Ken Brooks)

The age of the dinosaurs

Look to your right onto the beach, from the seaward end of the bridge over the railway line. Notice the rock outcrops and the nearby cliff of Little Galley Hill. These sandstone rocks are the remains of semi-tropical beaches, river beds and lagoons that once existed beside a vast freshwater sea that stretched south into what is now France, about 135 million years ago at the beginning of the Cretaceous age.

Had you lived then you would have seen tall tree-ferns, horsetails and other primitive vegetation on the swampy islands that provided food for a variety of animals. The rocks around Hastings are internationally important because of the survival in them of fossils from the beginning of the Cretaceous age, amongst which are small early mammals – our very distant ancestors.

Dinosaurs dominated the world then, and where Hastings lies was then much closer to the Equator and therefore quite hot. Since then our part of the crust of the Earth has moved northwards to a cooler latitude due to 'continental drift'. You would then have seen herds of dinosaurs lumbering about the beaches leaving footprints in the sand and mud as they sought food. By good fortune the natural fossilised casts of their footprints have survived and are quite often found in the rocks around Hastings and Bexhill, the most common footprints having been left by the Iguanadon, a plant eating animal up to 10 metres long, 4.5m high and weighing roughly 5 tonnes.

The footprints of clawed, flesh-eating dinosaurs have also been found, together with the remains of the fish, sharks, crocodiles and turtles that inhabited the rivers and swampy lagoons. Smaller creatures also existed, so the shells of gastropods are often found, together with occasional traces of clam shrimps, and even very rarely the remains of insects.

So, if you are lucky you too can find fossilised dinosaur bones on the beach. They are usually seen as rounded lumps of dark stone lying loose in the rock pools, the clue to their origin being the fine mesh of the bone marrow, amazingly preserved after such a long time. You can also find fossil plants, such as the blackened remains of wood, possibly burnt in fires in the Cretaceous forest that grew a long distance away towards where London now lies, and were washed down by the rivers to the ancient beaches. Even the solidified sand ripples of those beaches beside the Cretaceous sea can be found, looking just like the ripples of the modern beach.

Lefthand page: Local geologist Ken Brooks studies a footprint of an Iguanodon dinosaur on the beach east of Hastings. Similar footprints have been found at Bulverhythe.

A modern forest similar to the prehistoric forest
that grew at Bulverhythe around 2000 BC

Dr Peter Marsden taking samples of wood and peat from the
prehistoric forest for Carbon 14 dating and pollen study.
The wreck of the Amsterdam lies in the background

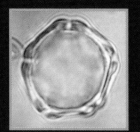

Left: Pollen of the Alder tree from Bulverhythe

Right: Hazel nut from the prehistoric forest

Lefthand page: A fallen tree 4000 years old in the forest at Bulverhythe

The prehistoric forest and the rising sea level

Eastward from the rocks off Little Galley Hill, towards Hastings, is a flat expanse of beach that initially looks fairly uninteresting. But examine it carefully and you will find large patches of peat and the logs from fallen trees. They were once the floor of a forest that existed here in prehistoric times when the sea level was more than 6 metres (20 feet) lower than it is today. If you are lucky you might even find a hazel nut or acorn! The wood and peat are not 'petrified', but have been preserved because they are buried in waterlogged ground. If they are allowed to dry out they simply shrink and split open, so need special conservation to preserve their form.

Samples have been dated by Carbon 14 to around 2000 BC – about the beginning of the Bronze Age, when people were developing farming. Pollen analysis has also shown that the forest was damp and fairly dense with alder trees, and that fern, sedge, grass bedstraw, dock, buttercup and bladderwort blanketed the forest floor. On the higher ground nearby were oak trees, with some birch, pine, lime, hazel and willow. There was even a little gorse, which still grows on Little Galley Hill.

Further inland scientists have also found buried peat dating back to 4000 BC, and pollen that shows that around 1000 BC the wooded valley had become largely meadow. This was evidently due to clearances by Iron Age farmers, since in the pollen were traces of cereal from crops that were being grown there!

The Combe Haven valley has also provided remarkable evidence of global warming over thousands of years. During an Ice Age, before 12,000 years ago, the sea level was over 100 m (roughly 300 feet) lower than today, and where the English Channel lies was once a landscape between England and France with an ancient meandering river flowing westwards to the Atlantic. The rivers on the modern English and French sides of the Channel, including the Rother and the Seine, were once its tributaries.

Scientists have sunk boreholes in the Combe Haven valley to find deeply buried ancient land surfaces which they have dated by Carbon 14. They found that about 9000 years ago the sea level was roughly 28 metres (90 feet) lower than it is today, and that the sea level has risen in stages, sometimes depositing clay, and at other times possibly sinking so as to allow a forest to grow and form peat. We are now living through a stage of rapid sea level rise, made more extreme by man's pollution of the atmosphere. Consequently, the submerged prehistoric forest and the massive sea defences at Bulverhythe reflect a dramatic story of global change whose future is difficult to forecast.

Wreck of the Amsterdam - what you can see

It seems bizarre that the wreck of the Amsterdam lies in the middle of the prehistoric forest. This heavily armed merchant ship of the Dutch East India Company, was run ashore by a mutinous crew on the 26th January 1749. It is the silt and peat filling the ancient Combe Haven valley that has remarkably preserved two-thirds of the ship, and made it the most complete East Indiaman known in the world. This vessel is protected by English Heritage since it is of exceptional international importance. She represents the East India companies of Europe that established global trade in the seventeenth and eighteenth centuries, and caused so much of the world to be explored and settled by European merchants. These ships normally carried silver, imported into Europe from Spanish Central America, and transported it to India, Indonesia, China and Japan so as to purchase spices, silks and porcelain for the European market.

The upper outline of the wreck, filled with sand and silt, is normally seen at the lowest monthly spring tides. The buried bottom of the ship lies about 8 metres (27 feet) down in the beach, and to reach it you would have to go down three deck levels. Because she quickly sank into the beach, much of her cargo, supplies and the possessions of the people on board are still in the ship.

Her bow faces the shore, but sadly this is being eroded by the sea. If you look at her end on you will notice that she is angled over towards the west, which means that more of the port (west) side survives than does her starboard (east) side. On the port side near the bow can often be seen a beam of the upper gun deck, whereas on the starboard side are the beams and supporting 'knees' of the lower gun deck.

Her stern is surrounded by iron sheet piles put there by Dutch archaeologists when they carried out trial excavations in the 1980's. A massive timber of the ship's stern on the starboard side can often be seen, showing how small this vessel is. Although only 44 metres (150 feet) long, she carried 333 people, and intended to sail from the Netherlands down the Atlantic to South Africa, then across the Indian Ocean to Jakarta in Java – a voyage of 11,000 miles that took from six to nine months. In her own time she was one of the largest ocean liners, but by our standards she was tiny!

The bow of the Amsterdam seen from above

Model of a Dutch East Indiaman from about 1750. The wreck survives up to the highest row of square gunports

Prehistoric forest 2000 BC

Stern

Lower gun deck knees

Posts: ? salvage shuttering of 1827

Fallen main mast

Upper deck beam

Bow

View of the features of the wreck that can often be seen at low spring tide

ATLANTIC
OCEAN

UK

Amsterdam

France

EUROPE

Spain

ASIA

China

Japa

AFRICA

India

INDIAN OCEAN

SOUTH
ATLANTIC
OCEAN

Java

Jakarta

EAST INDIES

Cape Town

AUSTRALIA

The intended voyage of the Amsterdam on her maiden voyage in 1749

The voyage, cargo and people

The story of the Amsterdam begins in the city of Amsterdam in 1748 when she was built in the shipyard of the Dutch East India Company (the Verenigde Oost-Indische Compagnie). Her captain, Willem Klump, was a man of thirty-three who lived with his wife Margareta and infant daughter Elysabet, and baby son Coenraad, in a tall narrow fronted house overlooking the tree-lined Prinsengracht. This was not his first voyage to the East Indies, so he knew the usual dangers that could be faced during the nine-month outward-bound voyage. But he could not be prepared for the tragedy of his next voyage. Although the main component of the ship's cargo was over two tonnes of silver bullion, she also carried a mixed cargo that included many bottles of wine and masses of fine cloth.

So, when she sailed out on her maiden voyage to Java, in November 1748, Captain Klump was in charge of 333 people, sailors, gunners, garrison soldiers and also five Company passengers three of whom were women. They had boarded the ship at Texel, at the northern entrance to the Zuyder Zee, but soon found that her voyage was delayed by westerly winds. When she eventually departed from the Dutch coast on 8 January 1749, Captain Klump did not immediately know that a member of his crew was diseased. But soon, as the confined conditions spread sickness, the crew began to die.

Left: Bottle of red wine from the Amsterdam

Middle: Silver ducatons from a twin ship to the Amsterdam, the Hollandia that was sunk in 1743

Right: Spanish silver Pieces-of-Eight from the wreck of the Hollandia. Captain Klump of the Amsterdam had two hundred to pay his costs for the voyage

Lead barrel from the Amsterdam, probably containing Irish butter

How she was wrecked

As the Amsterdam entered the English Channel she encountered a severe gale and struck the seabed so hard that her rudder was torn off. Captain Klump wanted to sail on to Portsmouth for repairs, and was even offered help by Captain Nicholas Wingfield from Hastings in his ship Roebuck. But the crew had other more urgent plans as fifty of their number were now dead from disease and forty more were sick and dying. They wanted to drive the ship ashore and escape.

There was a confrontation between the officers and the crew, discipline was lost and the crew broke into the cargo of wine to drown their miseries, so that when the ship was run ashore on the afternoon of Sunday, 26th January, someone on the shore heard the crew's drunken shouting. Archaeologists have found many wine bottles on the lower gun deck, and two fired lead musket balls showing that shooting had occurred. The bones of Adrian Welgevaren, probably the captain's cabin boy, were also found. Adrian was from the small Dutch market town of Leerdam, and ironically, the 26th January was his sixteenth birthday.

The ship was beached at high tide, and at low tide that Sunday night everyone managed to wade ashore through the cold, crashing waves, lit only by feeble candle lanterns. They abandoned their possessions, including two pet dogs, and Klump even left the ship's treasure unattended for a while. In the confusion some smugglers from Hastings secretly climbed on board and stole thirty silver ingots.

Archaeologists have found evidence of the chaos inside the ship, as books, clothing, gun equipment, food, boxes of wine bottles, medical equipment, rigging and guns are all mixed up on the lower gun deck.

Lefthand page: Reconstruction of the Amsterdam in the gale in January 1749 just before she was wrecked

The Amsterdam quickly sank into the beach at Bulverhythe, as this view of another Dutch ship shows

Swallowed in the beach

The excellent survival of two-thirds of the ship is due to her having sunk rapidly through the prehistoric forest and deep into the clay filling the ancient river valley. The chests of silver were saved, together with some wine and cloth, but most other salvage was stopped when the man responsible blew himself up. His name was Christopher Nutt, and his remains are buried in St. Clement's Church in Hastings. Eventually, the Dutch East India Company decided to abandon salvage and on 3 April 1749, resolved to sell the ship and its contents, though there is no record that such a sale took place.

5 bronze guns of 1748 from the wreck have the A-VOC insignia of the Dutch East India Co

Model of a Dutch East Indiaman like the Amsterdam

The wreck is two-thirds complete and survives to her upper row of gunports

Later salvage attempts

The Amsterdam has been a tourist attraction in the beach of Hastings since George Wooll of Hastings referred to her story in a local visitor guide that he published in 1827. Interest in the wreck remains, and even today old local fishing families still tell stories handed down over more than two centuries, of the plague that infected her crew.

Attempts have been made by treasure hunters to salvage the wreck, the first in 1810 when soldiers of the King's German Legion, quartered at Bexhill, encountered flowing sand, and found little.

Next, in February 1827, poor labourers dug into the bow with greater success for they found glass goblets and wine glasses, square glass gin bottles, a cask of knives, and a pair of scales. These achieved such high prices at auction that the Lord Warden of the Cinque Ports, who had rights over local shipwrecks, decided to claim much of the profit from future salvage work. This stopped further salvage, except in April 1827 when a company of shareholders tried again, but without success.

Finally, in 1969 some workmen building a new sewer outfall nearby, used mechanical excavators to dig into the wreck at low tide. They found bronze cannons dated 1748, pewter tableware, bottles of wine, cloth, military equipment, clay pipes, rigging, barrels, and many personal possessions. Archaeologists, horrified at the damage, quickly began investigating the wreck, and sought its protection as an historic site.

Top left: A family group visiting the Amsterdam in 1912

Middle left: One of the earliest known photographs of the Amsterdam, 13 May 1911

Bottom left: Mechanical excavators digging into the ship's stern in 1969

Right: The lower half of a gunport and the upper gun deck exposed in 1969

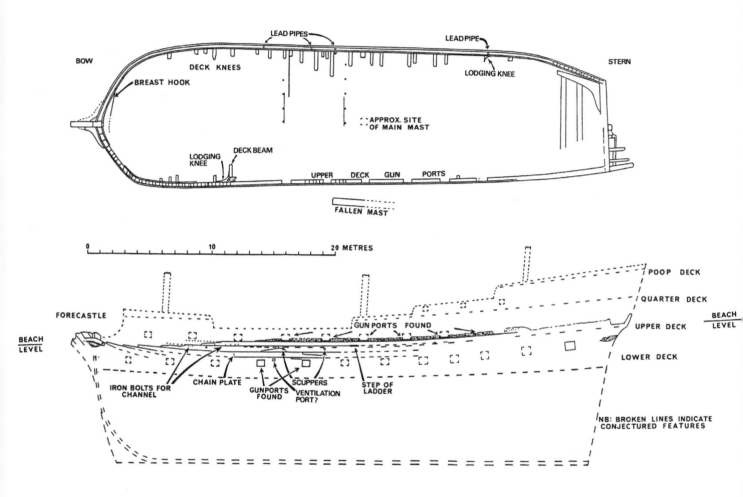

A plan and reconstructed side elevation of the remains of the Amsterdam, drawn from the archaeological survey in 1969, with additions from excavations in 1984

Protection and investigation

During 1969 – 1970 English archaeologists and Dutch historians worked hard to find the true story of this ship: when, why and how she was wrecked, and how much of her and her contents had survived. Peter Marsden discovered that two-thirds of the ship had survived, together with a large proportion of her contents, and Joop Reinboud found her story in the Dutch archives.

Protection for the ship as an historic monument was impossible then as no relevant law existed. Consequently, a campaign was mounted by archaeologists for the creation of such a law, and the Amsterdam was featured prominently in British newspapers, and her status was discussed in Parliament. Other historic wrecks also needed protection, particularly the Mary Rose sunk off Portsmouth in 1545. As a result the Protection of Wrecks Act 1973 was passed by Parliament, and the Amsterdam was one of the first to be protected under the new law.

Since the Dutch government owned the wreck, the British archaeologists decided to offer the ship and her contents back to the Dutch people if they wanted them. For some years a publicity campaign was carried out in Holland, with the result that in 1974–5 Dutch colleagues established the 'Foundation for the East India Company Ship Amsterdam' (Stichting VOC–schip Amsterdam) with the support of Amsterdam City Council.

After ten years of investigation the Foundation began limited underwater excavations using Dutch and British diving archaeologists led by Jerzey Gawronski, Jon Adams and Peter Marsden. Also, a feasibility study was completed to establish how she could be excavated, raised, transported back to Amsterdam, conserved and displayed. Technically, it was possible, but the cost was found to be so great that the scheme was abandoned.

When in 2005 the protection of the wreck came under care of English Heritage, its long term safety in situ began to be considered. By coincidence the local authorities around Hastings agreed in 2005 to include the wreck site in the proposed Pebsham Countryside Park in the Combe Haven valley. At long last there was beginning to be a framework whereby the British and Dutch authorities could work together to preserve this unique but somewhat neglected wreck that has suffered serious damage since 1969.

View of the Amsterdam looking forward towards the shore

An archaeologist measures the ship's port side in 1969

Careful drawings of objects are made by artists to record the contents of the wreck

The surveys of the ship are drawn as the first stage in reconstruct what the ship looked like

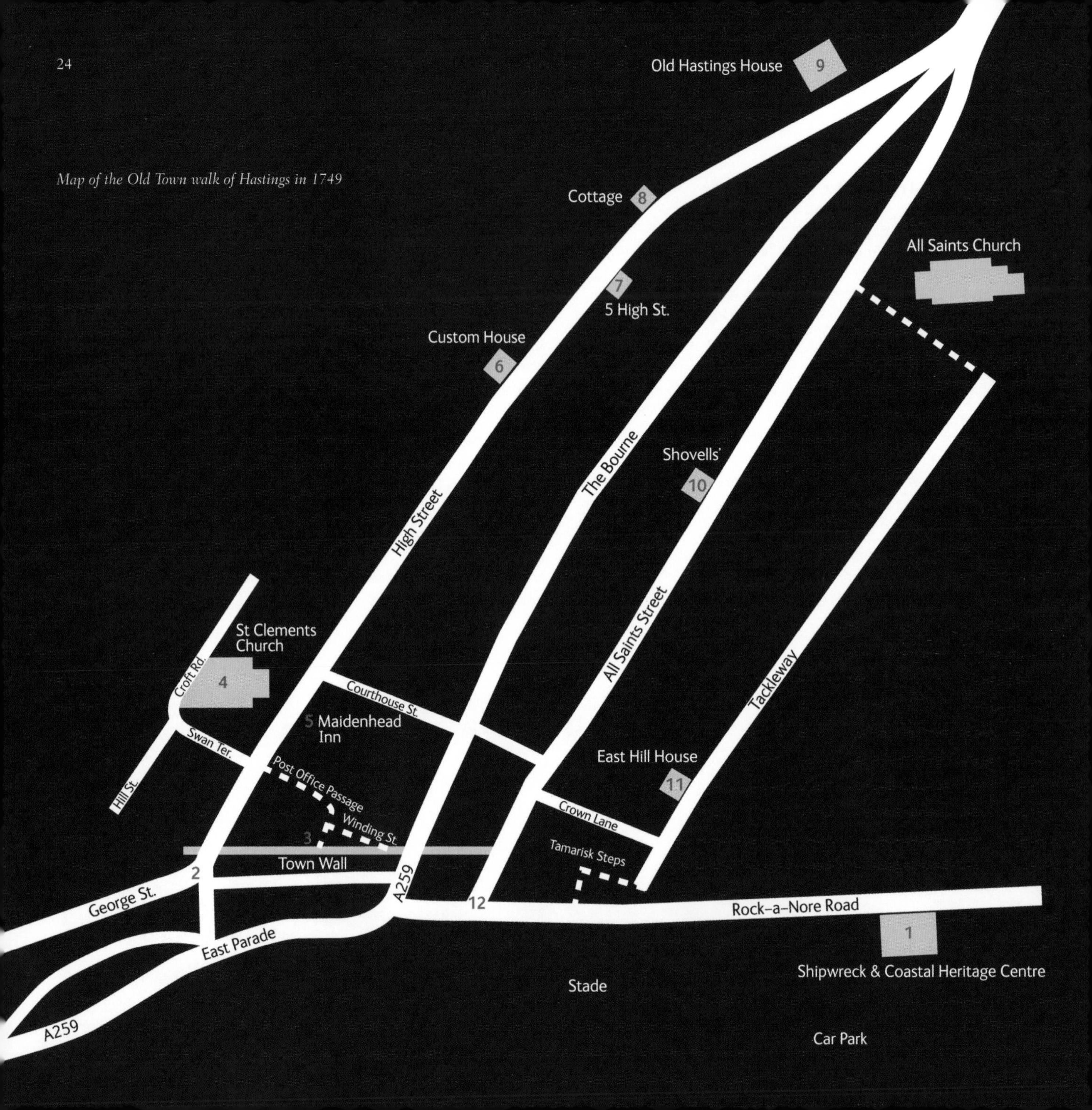

Map of the Old Town walk of Hastings in 1749

Old Hastings House **9**

Cottage **8**

7
5 High St.

All Saints Church

Custom House
6

The Bourne

Shovells'
10

High Street

St Clements
Church

Croft Rd.

4

Courthouse St.

All Saints Street

Tackleway

5 Maidenhead
Inn

Swan Ter.

Hill St.

Post Office Passage

East Hill House

11

Winding St.

3

Crown Lane

Town Wall

A259

Tamarisk Steps

2

George St.

12

Rock–a–Nore Road

1

East Parade

A259

Stade

Shipwreck & Coastal Heritage Centre

Car Park

3. The inner face of the defensive wall of Hastings preserved in Winding Street

3. The outer face of the town's defensive wall off Winding Street

Guided tour of Hastings 1749

Although the drama of the shipwreck lay in the beach at Bulverhythe, it was in nearby Hastings that the Dutch survivors stayed before returning home, and where the treasure from the Amsterdam was stored. Hastings was then a small fishing port lying in the narrow Bourne valley, and nowadays, you can walk around the 'Old Town' to visit places that are part of the story of the ship. You can also see some of the treasures from the wreck at the Shipwreck and Coastal Heritage Centre at the back of Hastings harbour, by the tall net sheds in Rock-a-Nore Road. The tour starts at the Centre –

1. Walk west from the SHIPWRECK & COASTAL HERITAGE CENTRE along Rock-a-Nore Road, following the old beach line at the base of the cliffs, to the seaward end of the High Street in the medieval 'Old Town' of Hastings.

2. At the junction of the HIGH STREET and George Street, you are standing on what was the beach in 1749 where fishermen hauled up their boats and sold their fish. George Street was then a beach road with a row of fishermen's cottages facing the sea.

   This is part of the medieval Cinque Port of Hastings, a town that provided ships and men for the King's naval service in medieval times, for which it received certain rights. For over eight hundred years its High Street was the main highway to London, though the town itself originally extended further seawards, but part of it was washed away in storms during the thirteenth century. It was only when the present harbour arm was built around 1900 that the present beach was formed on the south side of the A259 main road where there are now amusements.

3. In 1749 a substantial stone defensive town wall crossed the bottom of the Old Town valley, protecting Hastings from enemy naval attacks. You will notice a plaque on the side of the High Street marking the site of its Seagate, though the date given on the plaque is now disputed. The remains of the defensive wall are nowadays almost lost within recent seafront buildings, but a portion can be seen if you walk a few yards up the High Street to POST OFFICE PASSAGE, on the right. Continue down the passage to WINDING STREET, and turn right to the lower corner of the street, and enter the gate into a paved area beside the TOWN WALL.

   Nobody knows when the defensive wall was built, though it certainly existed in the sixteenth century when it defended the town against French attacks, and subsequently against Spanish and Dutch attacks.

4. St. Clements church where Evensong was in progress when the Amsterdam was run ashore on Sunday 26 January 1749

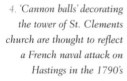

4. 'Cannon balls' decorating the tower of St. Clements church are thought to reflect a French naval attack on Hastings in the 1790's

5. Spoons from the wreck have the initials of Andries van Bockom and his wife Pieternella

4. Return to the HIGH STREET, and look at St. CLEMENT'S CHURCH. It was here that the people of Hastings first heard the Amsterdam in distress on 26 January 1749. A letter to John Collier in Bath, relates that "She came in Sunday 3 a clock in the afternoon, while the people was at Church, with firing a great many guns". In the church is a magnificent monument to John Collier (we shall return to him later); and in an unmarked grave in the churchyard are the remains of Christopher Nutt who blew himself up whilst trying to salvage the ship during 1749.

Notice the 'cannon balls' set into the outer face of the church tower on either side of the upper window. One was apparently fired by a French warship in the 1790's, and remains there as a local trophy, and the other cannon ball was carved in stone to balance the 'design'.

5. Walk up the High Street to the corner of COURTHOUSE STREET. On its seaward side and fronting onto the High Street is a group of modern shops that were built on the site of the MAIDENHEAD INN after it was destroyed by bombing during World War II.

The three Dutch women from the Amsterdam stayed at the Maidenhead Inn immediately after the ship was wrecked. They were the sisters Pieternella van Bockom Schook, who had just married Andries van Bockom, a 25 year old Junior Merchant, and her 22 year old sister Catharina. Some of their possessions have been found in the wreck, including a fan, shoes, a silk petticoat and spoons with the initials PBS and AB. A local person called them "very fine women". The other woman from the Amsterdam was Maria Monk, the 33 year old wife of Jacob Hal, a Company army lieutenant. She was illiterate and of a lower social rank. Captain Klump probably stayed at the Maidenhead too, and would have paid the bills with some of the 200 Spanish silver Pieces-of-Eight that he had been given for the ship's expenses.

4. Lefthand page: Hill Street and St. Clements church are little different from what they were like in 1749

6. Walk further up the High Street to the site of the CUSTOM HOUSE, sadly demolished in the 1960's and replaced by modern houses at Philip Cole Close. The corner of the Custom House, of red bricks and stone, fortunately survives and is a reminder of where over 2 tons of silver bullion from the Amsterdam was stored under the watchful eye of Mr. Coppard, the local Customs Officer.

The total value of the bullion was then almost £30,000 (the value in 2000 would be over £3 million). Thomas Smith wrote to John Collier in Bath that of the "28 chest of silver, 27 are lodged in the Custom House, but what value in each chest is unknown, but some of them is as much as two men can carry. The one chest as was missing is since found, but empty." A few days later John Collier's secretary, Richard Patrick, wrote "On Mr. Whitfield's arrival he had it cried round the town, if any person or persons who had taken any of these wedges of silver and would bring the same to him, they should have 40 shillings per wedge [the value in 2000 was over £200 each] and no questions asked. Otherwise, in case they were found guilty, they would be severely punished. Several of these silver wedges have been delivered to Mr. Whitfield, but am afraid he will never be able to get the whole, as a great many of those fellows carry such vile principals, for had not several of these creatures offered the silver for sale. I question whether this affair would have been discovered". The ship's treasure was eventually sent to London, and was then shipped back to Amsterdam city.

7. Smuggling contraband from France was one of the most lucrative occupations of the people of Hastings during the eighteenth century, because of the very high taxes imposed by the government on imported tea, brandy, gin, tobacco, salt, sugar, snuff and silk. Some respectable families in Hastings even financed the smuggling by the poor fishing folk.

Thomas Moore, a wealthy property owner, and his family may have done this, for he owned a part share in a local sailing ship. When his widow, Joanna, died in 1757 at 5 HIGH STREET, probable evidence of smuggled goods was discarded in her garden. These included a surprising number of teapots and teacups from the 1740's, and pottery from Normandy. They were found in archaeological excavations in 2000 and indicate an excessive use of highly taxed tea drinking, and contact with the local people of northern France.

6. *The old Custom House in the High Street (courtesy of Hastings Museum) where the Amsterdam's treasure was stored. This was, sadly, demolished in the 1960's*

6. *The surviving corner of the old Custom House*

8. A cottage at the top of the High Street

*8. A tiny 'squint' window in the cottage gives a
view down the High Street to the sea*

*9. Old Hastings House, the home of John Collier, whose letters
tell us so much about the loss of the Amsterdam*

8. At the top end of the high walk overlooking the High Street is a small COTTAGE with a squint window enabling the occupant inside to look down the entire length of the High Street – ideal for knowing what was going on if you were a smuggler!

9. A little beyond this, at the very top of the High Street, is OLD HASTINGS HOUSE, the fine Georgian home built by John Collier, a highly respected and very wealthy solicitor during the eighteenth century. He was town Clerk of Hastings, five times Mayor, agent for the Duke of Newcastle, Surveyor–General of the customs of Kent, and was very much involved in stopping smuggling.

But in January 1749 he was in Bath recovering from gout, paralysis and a stroke, and it was because of this that we know so much about the Amsterdam. Various people wrote to him, including the Mayor of Hastings, William Thorpe, who complained that "the care of the sick Dutchmen, the plague of quartering soldiers [guarding the wreck], their and others thieving, has engrossed my whole time." He concluded that "The wine [from the Amsterdam] is French. If you would have any, please let me know. I fancy about 1 shilling [about £5 in 2000] will be the price."

10. Cross the main A259 road, The Bourne, where the ancient town stream flowed, to ALL SAINTS STREET, a medieval road that extends southwards from All Saints Church. Stop outside the quaint old house called SHOVELLS. You are now in the poor fishermen's quarter of the town of 1749, and many old houses, like Shovells, retain their centuries old timber-framed frontages, unlike most houses in the High Street that were fashionably rebuilt or re-fronted in the later eighteenth century. Many of the people who tried to plunder the wreck would have lived in All Saints Street. Richard Patrick, secretary to John Collier, wrote "The soldiers [guarding the wreck] have shot a man indiscreetly at this wreck, and Mr Tilden, as Coroner for the Rape of Hastings, has been applied to upon the affair, to summon a jury to view the body and to enquire into the death of this person. But as Mr. Tilden is laid up with a fit of the gout, he desired me to act as his deputy." Richard Patrick consulted several people, and decided not to get involved: "the death of this person was not to be enquired into by the Coroner and jury, by reason he was killed at sea, ten or fifteen roads below high water mark."

11. Near the bottom of All Saints Street is the passage named STARR'S COTTAGES. It leads up to EAST HILL HOUSE, built by the Wenham family partly from the profits of smuggling, piracy and privateering in the eighteenth century. In 1775 George Wenham married Martha Hide, whose father, Adam, had been arrested for piracy off Hastings in August 1758. He was in partnership with Nicholas Wingfield in the ship Roebuck when they boarded a Dutch vessel and stole casks of Irish butter. In the following year Wingfield and Hide were publicly executed by hanging on the foreshore of the River Thames at Wapping, in east London. This was the same Wingfield who in 1749 had offered to help Captain Klump to sail the Amsterdam to safety.

When in 1788 James Wenham was arrested for seizing another vessel and its cargo of gin and brandy, his brother and a friend stood bail for him of £2000 – a huge amount of money then, and James was fined £729.

12. End your walk at the bottom of All Saints Street where it joins Rock-a-Nore Road, and return to the Shipwreck and Coastal Heritage Centre.

10. 'Shovells' is one of many ancient houses in All Saints Street

The logo of the Centre depicts a sinking sailing ship like the Amsterdam.

Entrance to the Centre

Income from the Centre's shop helps to preserve the history of the unique maritime shore of Hastings.

Visit the Shipwreck & Coastal Heritage Centre, Rock-a-Nore Road

You enter the Shipwreck and Coastal Heritage Centre through a reconstruction of the side of the Amsterdam with one of her original iron cannons, found on the seabed off Bexhill. Inside are many treasures from the ship including bottles of wine, pulley blocks, pewter spoons, samples of the ship's cargo of cloth, and even two fired musket balls. There are also original silver Pieces-of-Eight and ducatons from a similar Dutch East Indiaman, and you will see the bones of Adrian Welgevaren, the sixteen year old lad who was probably Captain Klump's cabin boy. These bones were once taken to his family church in Leerdam, Netherlands, but burial was not possible as the graveyard is paved over. There are hundreds of other objects from the wreck, from pins to pipes, and there are even pieces of the ship. This is the only permanent exhibition about the ship, though many objects from the wreck are stored in the city of Amsterdam, particularly at the Dutch national maritime museum, the Nederlands Scheepvaartmuseum.

The wreck has survived partly because the sandstone rocks nearby form a beach breakwater stopping erosion. It is amidst these rocks that you can sometimes find loose dinosaur bones and other Cretaceous fossils. The exhibition at the Centre includes locally found dinosaur bones from various parts of the beaches in the Hastings area, as well as a natural footprint of an Iguanodon dinosaur preserved in sandstone, parts of fossil fish and plants, and even the 'poo' from sharks, all clues to what the beach was like 135 million years ago!

The Amsterdam had sunk into a prehistoric forest that was growing on the shore 3,500 – 4000 years ago, and the exhibition includes plant remains preserved by the waterlogged ground, and prehistoric tools from around the time the forest was growing. There is also an explanation of how the sea level has been rising and changing the coastline over thousands of years, and how it is likely to affect people in the future.

Other exhibits include discoveries from the English warship Anne abandoned in 1690 in the local beach nearby off Pett Level after suffering damage by the French navy. There are also hundreds of bottles of Cognac and other items from the Danish sailing ship Thomas Lawrence sunk in a collision off Hastings in 1862 whilst bound for the Danish Virgin Islands. Ammunition is exhibited from the World War 2 wreck of the S.S. Storaa, a merchant ship that was sunk by an enemy torpedo in 1943 with the deaths of twenty-one of her British and Danish crew. Her story is told, with underwater photographs, because the museum supported pleas for her protection as a war grave by the Ministry of Defence. The wrecks of the Anne and Thomas Lawrence are now owned by the museum trust, and are protected by English Heritage.

The spectacular audio-visual show in the museum theatre gives a vivid account of this unique maritime coast, whilst the well-stocked museum shop provides a range of nautical souvenirs for all the family. The museum is run by a charitable trust, and depends upon donations for its income to maintain the preservation of the local historic wrecks, and to help the trust run its educational programme.

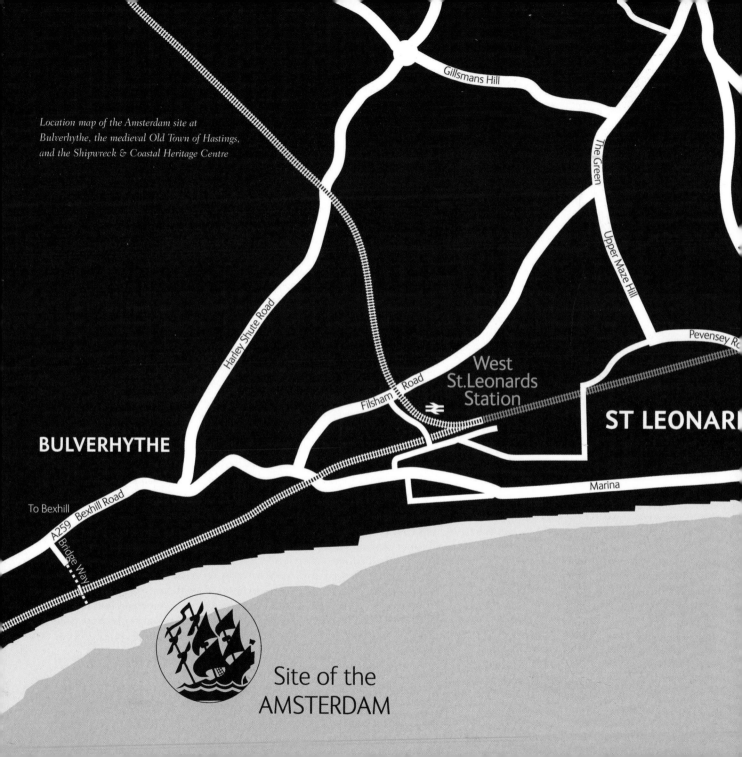

Location map of the Amsterdam site at Bulverhythe, the medieval Old Town of Hastings, and the Shipwreck & Coastal Heritage Centre

Gillsmans Hill

The Green

Upper Maze Hill

Harley Shutte Road

Pevensey Rd

West St.Leonards Station

Filsham Road

BULVERHYTHE

ST LEONARI

Marina

To Bexhill Bexhill Road

A259

Bridge Way

Site of the
AMSTERDAM

Acknowledgments

The Nautical Museums Trust is grateful to the Environment Agency and the Local Heritage Initiative of the Heritage Lottery Fund for financing this booklet, and to Sarah Fretwell, publication designer, and Kevin Boorman of Hastings Borough Council for their help. Thanks are also due to Hastings Museum, Hastings Reference Library and Ken Brooks for permission to reproduce illustrations on pages 11, 21 and 28. Otherwise the text and photographs are by Peter Marsden.

The Nautical Museums Trust

is a registered charity founded in 1982 to encourage the preservation of maritime history for educational purposes. The Trust achieves this by maintaining a government accredited maritime museum, the Shipwreck & Coastal Heritage Centre in Hastings, and by organising educational events. It also owns and manages three historic shipwrecks on the seabed near Hastings: the English warships Anne of 1690, off Pett Level, and the Resolution of 1703, off Pevensey; and the Danish sailing ship Thomas Lawrence sunk off Hastings in 1862. Within the museum is preserved the last Rye barge, Primrose, a traditional nineteenth century vessel that was rescued from the River Rother.

The Trust relies upon the generosity of its supporters and on donations from visitors to its museum, as well as on income from the museum shop.

For further information please contact the museum Manager on **01424 437452**, or visit the web site **www.shipwreck-heritage.org.uk**